Making Friends

By Janine Amos and Annabel Spenceley

Consultant Rachael Underwood

CHERRYTREE BOOKS

A CHERRYTREE BOOK

This edition first published in 2007
By Cherrytree Books, part of
The Evans Publishing Group Limited
2a Portman Mansions
Chiltern Street
London W1U 6NR

Printed in China

British Library Cataloguing in Publication Data

Amos, Janine
  Making friends. - Rev. ed. - (Growing up)
  1. Friendship - Pictorial works - Juvenile literature
  2. Social interaction - Pictorial works - Juvenile
literature
  I. Title
  302.3'4

ISBN 9781842344897

CREDITS
Editor: Louise John
Designer: D.R.ink
Photography: Gareth Boden
Production: Jenny Mulvanny

Based on the original edition of Making Friends published in 1997

With thanks to: Megan and Sonia Sear, Olivia Varley, Kirsty and Connor Sweeney, Kellah-Monique Henry, Aman Jutla and Moya Saunders.

Splashing in Puddles

Splash!
It's been raining.

Megan is jumping
in a puddle.

5

Megan sees a girl.

"Snap!" says Megan.
"You've got boots on too.
You can splash with me."

Olivia goes to the puddle.

She jumps with Megan.

Megan's mum smiles at them.
"You've made friends,"
she says.

Building a House

The children are building a house.

Kellah is
watching.

13

Kellah pushes the blocks.

The house tumbles down.

"Don't do that," shouts Moya. "Now we have to build it again."

How do you think
Moya feels?
How does Kellah feel?

Kellah walks away.

Bryony follows her.

"You seem unhappy,"
says Bryony.

"Did you
want to play?"

Kellah nods her head.

"If you'd like to join in,
you can," says Bryony.
"Tell the children what
you want."

"You come too,"
says Kellah.

They go over to the blocks.

"Can I play, please?" Kellah says to the children.

"Put some blocks on
the roof," Moya tells her.

Kellah builds the roof with Moya.

They work together.

Moya smiles at her. "You're my friend," she says.

How does Kellah
feel now?

Teachers' Notes

The following extension activities will assist teachers in delivering aspects of the PSHE and Citizenship Framework as well as aspects of the Healthy Schools criteria.

Specific areas supported are:

- Framework for PSHE&C 1a, 1b, 2a, 2c, 3a, 4a, 4b, 5d, 5f, 5g
- National Healthy School Criteria 1.1

Activity for *Splashing in Puddles*

Read the story to the children.

- With the children sitting in a circle, ask them to identify how Megan's mum can tell the girls have made friends. (If need be, look at the last two pictures again).
- Ask the children what it was that helped Olivia and Megan make friends.
- Explain that Olivia and Megan are 'puddle splashing' friends – they like to do the same thing and it makes them laugh and feel happy.
- Ask all the children to stand up if they like splashing in puddles. Get the standing children to form a circle by holding hands. Point out that anyone else in the circle could be their friend for puddle splashing. Seat the children again and this time ask all the children to stand up who like to play football. Ask them to make a circle by holding hands and tell them that anyone in the circle can be their football friend. Seat the children again.
- Repeat with a range of different activities getting the children to see how many other children share their tastes in 'fun' things to do.
- Draw two large circles on the board. Label one yes and the other no. Write the names of 6 different children from the group on small cards. Attach them to the board. Ask the other children to suggest an activity the named children might like doing. Sort the name cards into the yes or no circle by asking the children concerned if they do or don't like the activity. Repeat several times allowing children to take turns to sort and stick the cards.

Activity for *Building a House*

Read the story to the children.

- Ask the children why they think Kellah pushed the bricks over.
- Ask them why Moya was angry.
- Explain to the children that when we play games we have rules to make the game easier to understand for everyone. Kellah wanted to play knocking down the bricks but Moya wanted to play building a house.
- Ask the children who was wrong, Kellah or Moya? Why?
- Explain that when we start playing a game together we can make up the rules together but when we join in someone else's game we need to play by their rules or ask them to do things differently.
- Ask the children if they have ever made a mistake when they were playing with someone and didn't understand the rules.